PRAYERS FOR

Families

BARBOUR
PUBLISHING

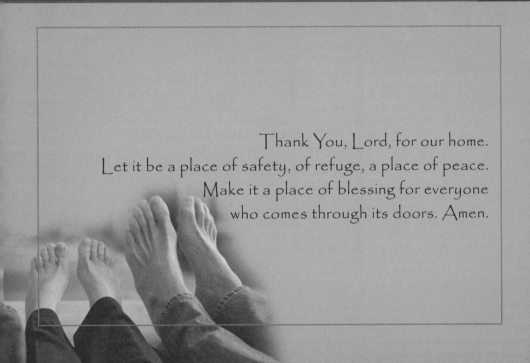

Thank You, Lord, for our home.
Let it be a place of safety, of refuge, a place of peace.
Make it a place of blessing for everyone
who comes through its doors. Amen.

Everything good comes from You, Lord.
And everything You do is good. Thank You
for Your obvious blessings, and thank You for the
things that don't look like blessings now. We trust
that You are bringing good into our lives today.
Amen.

Lord, we come to You together, to thank You for our marriage. Keep our love strong; help us to support each other and to look to You when things are tough. Help us to love unselfishly and to honor You even in our marriage.

Amen.

Children, obey your parents in everything, for this pleases the Lord.

COLOSSIANS 3:20 NIV

Dear God, I am going to tell the truth because I know it makes You happy.

Amen.

How can we profess faith in God's Word and then refuse to let it inspire and direct our thinking, our activity, our decisions, and our responsibilities toward one another?

POPE JOHN PAUL II

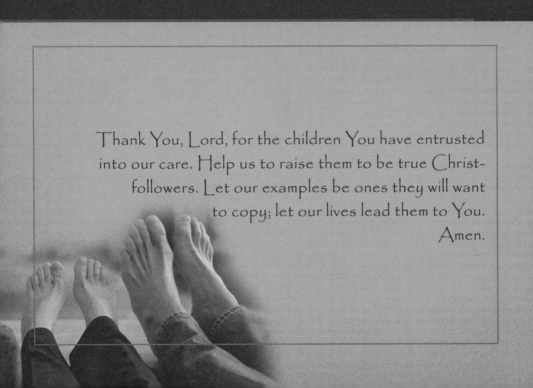

Thank You, Lord, for the children You have entrusted into our care. Help us to raise them to be true Christ-followers. Let our examples be ones they will want to copy; let our lives lead them to You.

Amen.

Lord, help me to listen today.
Amen.

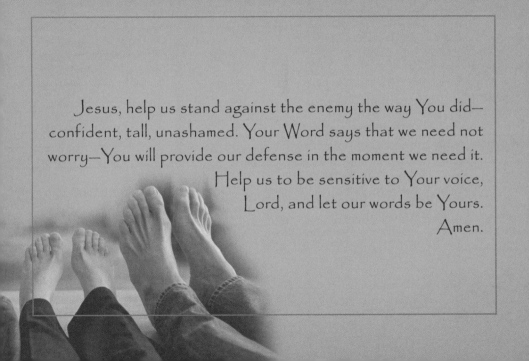

Jesus, help us stand against the enemy the way You did—confident, tall, unashamed. Your Word says that we need not worry—You will provide our defense in the moment we need it. Help us to be sensitive to Your voice, Lord, and let our words be Yours. Amen.

Father, please protect our children from spiritual and physical harm, and give them sound minds and bodies. We thank You in advance for answered prayers.
Amen.

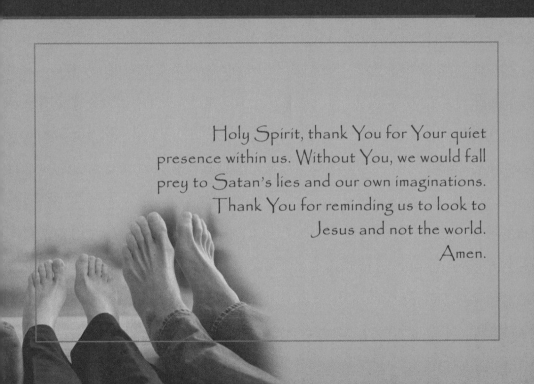

Holy Spirit, thank You for Your quiet presence within us. Without You, we would fall prey to Satan's lies and our own imaginations. Thank You for reminding us to look to Jesus and not the world.

Amen.

*Friends love through all kinds of weather,
and families stick together in all kinds of trouble.*

PROVERBS 17:17 MSG

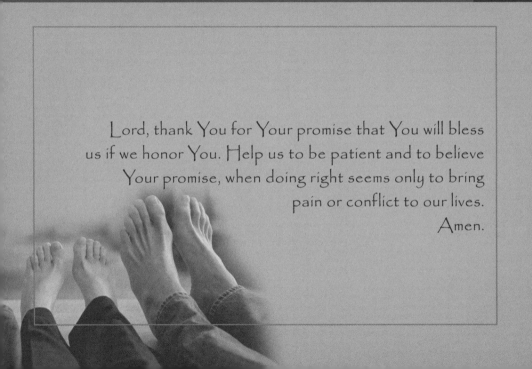

Lord, thank You for Your promise that You will bless us if we honor You. Help us to be patient and to believe Your promise, when doing right seems only to bring pain or conflict to our lives.

Amen.

Jesus, thank You for loving little children.
Help me to trust You as fully as my kids do,
with the childlike faith You desire.
Amen.

Your hands made me and formed me;
give me understanding to learn your commands.

PSALM 119:73 NIV

Jesus, some of my friends don't know You.
Help me show them that You love them and
that they can have You live in their hearts, too.
Amen.

Father, sometimes we say things that should never have left our lips. Lord, help us to fully humble ourselves in confession before You and before each other. Heal our hurts and help us to forgive each other. Amen.

True love doesn't consist of holding hands;
it consists of holding hearts.

O. A. BATTISTA

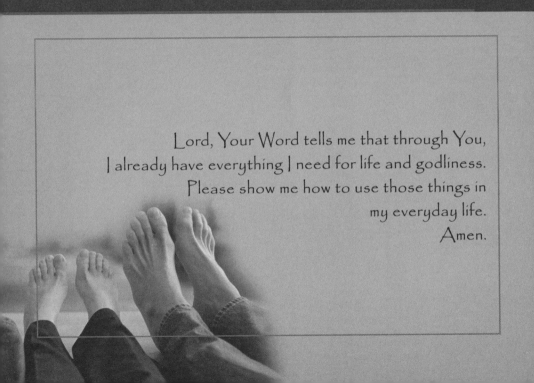

Lord, Your Word tells me that through You,
I already have everything I need for life and godliness.
Please show me how to use those things in
my everyday life.
Amen.

Father God, thank You for Your provision
for our family. You provide everything we need,
and we acknowledge Your great goodness.
Amen.

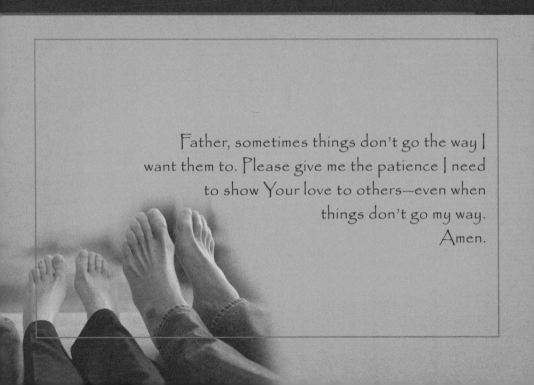

Father, sometimes things don't go the way I
want them to. Please give me the patience I need
to show Your love to others—even when
things don't go my way.
Amen.

O God! What amazing creatures You have fashioned in my children! I watch them as they grow and I see reflections of me, yes, but, thank You, Lord; I see reflections of You, too. As they grow, Lord, help me to groom them to show more of You and less of me. Help us to honor You always with our lives. Amen.

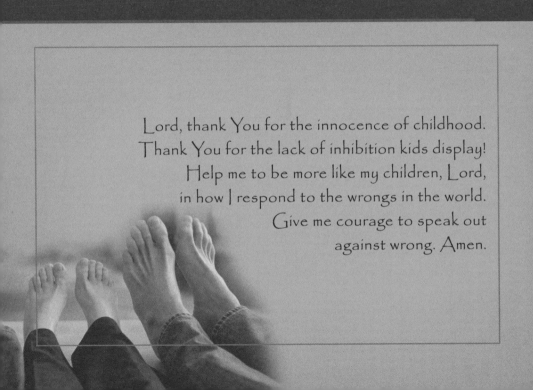

Lord, thank You for the innocence of childhood.
Thank You for the lack of inhibition kids display!
Help me to be more like my children, Lord,
in how I respond to the wrongs in the world.
Give me courage to speak out
against wrong. Amen.

Fix these words of mine in your hearts and minds. . . . Teach them to your children, talking about them when you sit at home and when you walk along the road, when you lie down and when you get up. Write them on the doorframes of your houses and on your gates.

DEUTERONOMY 11:18-20 NIV

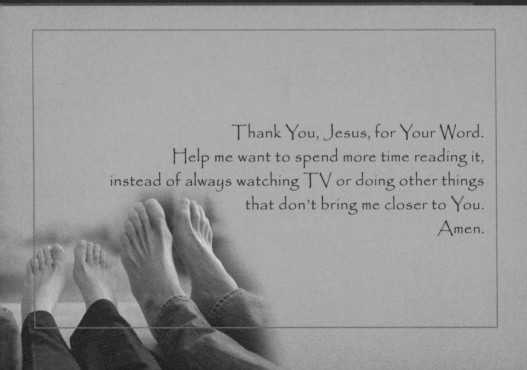

Thank You, Jesus, for Your Word.
Help me want to spend more time reading it,
instead of always watching TV or doing other things
that don't bring me closer to You.
Amen.

Help me know how to discipline my children, Lord. Help me teach them to make right choices in the future, not because I said they should behave a certain way, but because their hearts are drawn to what is right. Amen.

Lord, keep me from being too proud
to admit to my kids when I've been wrong.
Let me be honest and open with them,
so that they know it's okay to be honest
and open with me. Amen.

God, thank You for delivering us today! We saw Your presence in a mighty way as You protected us from harm. Thank You for Your constant love and never-failing attention. Amen.

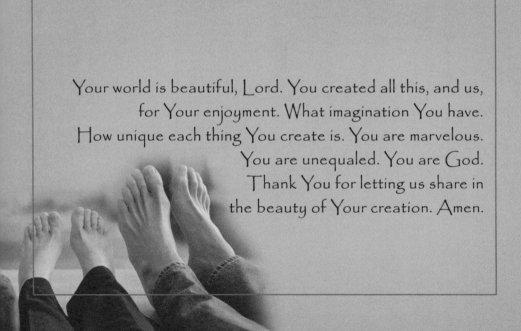

Your world is beautiful, Lord. You created all this, and us, for Your enjoyment. What imagination You have. How unique each thing You create is. You are marvelous. You are unequaled. You are God. Thank You for letting us share in the beauty of Your creation. Amen.

To us, family means putting your arms around each other and being there.

BARBARA BUSH

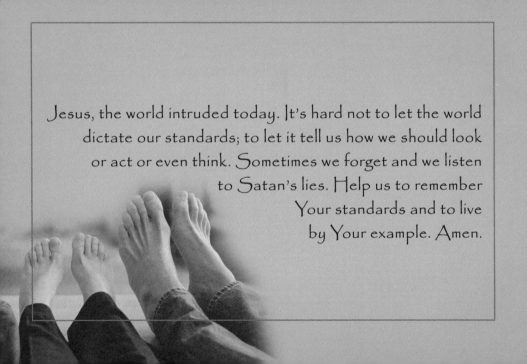

Jesus, the world intruded today. It's hard not to let the world dictate our standards; to let it tell us how we should look or act or even think. Sometimes we forget and we listen to Satan's lies. Help us to remember Your standards and to live by Your example. Amen.

Lord, thank You for the lessons You teach us through our children. Amen.

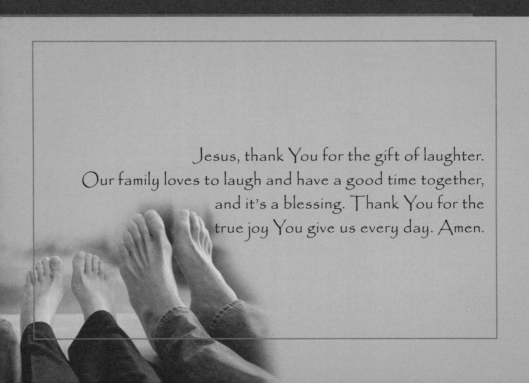

Jesus, thank You for the gift of laughter.
Our family loves to laugh and have a good time together,
and it's a blessing. Thank You for the
true joy You give us every day. Amen.

God, forgiving someone who's hurt me is really hard to do. Please help me forgive this person completely, the way You've forgiven me. Amen.

Help us to trust You even when nothing makes sense. Give us wisdom; help us make the best choices in new situations. Amen.

God-loyal people, living honest lives,
make it much easier for their children.

PROVERBS 20:7 MSG

Lord, help us to discipline wisely. Help us not "provoke [them] to wrath," Lord. Let our decisions make them stronger, not discourage or dishearten them. Help us always point the way to You, even in our discipline.

Amen.

God, thank You for the ability to learn new things. Please bless the teachers and other educators that spend time teaching my family. Help me to always remember that true wisdom is found in loving and obeying You. Amen.

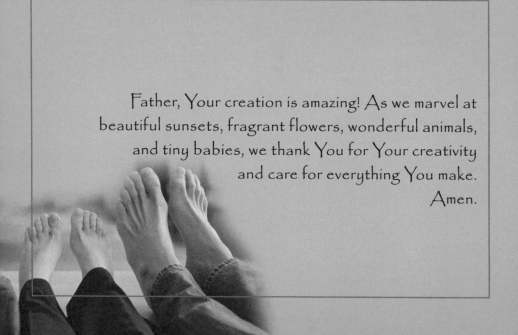

Father, Your creation is amazing! As we marvel at beautiful sunsets, fragrant flowers, wonderful animals, and tiny babies, we thank You for Your creativity and care for everything You make.
Amen.

Through the LORD's mercies we are not consumed, because His compassions fail not. They are new every morning; great is Your faithfulness.

LAMENTATIONS 3:22-23 NKJV

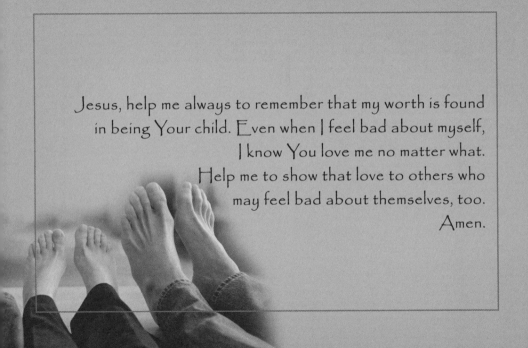

Jesus, help me always to remember that my worth is found in being Your child. Even when I feel bad about myself, I know You love me no matter what. Help me to show that love to others who may feel bad about themselves, too. Amen.

Just because I loves you—that's da reason why ma soul is full of color like da wings of a butterfly.

LANGSTON HUGHES

O Lord, You have blessed us so much, with so many things. Let us use Your gifts wisely and bless others through what You have given us.

Amen.

Father, thank You for spiritual leaders that show us an earthly example of living for You. Please bless these people in our lives and let them know we are praying for them. Amen.

God, please protect our family—those of us
who live nearby and others who are far away.
Keep us bound together in Your love
now and always.
Amen.

Lord, we give this new day to You. Each of us has somewhere to be, something to do. Help us honor You in our words and actions today, and bring us back together safely this evening. Thank You for the love we share. Thank You for family. Amen.

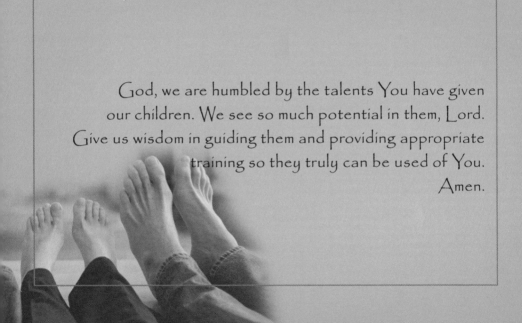

God, we are humbled by the talents You have given
our children. We see so much potential in them, Lord.
Give us wisdom in guiding them and providing appropriate
training so they truly can be used of You.

Amen.

Husbands, go all out in your love for your wives, exactly as Christ did for the church—a love marked by giving, not getting. Christ's love makes the church whole. His words evoke her beauty. Everything he does and says is designed to bring the best out of her. . . . And that is how husbands ought to love their wives.

EPHESIANS 5:25-28 MSG

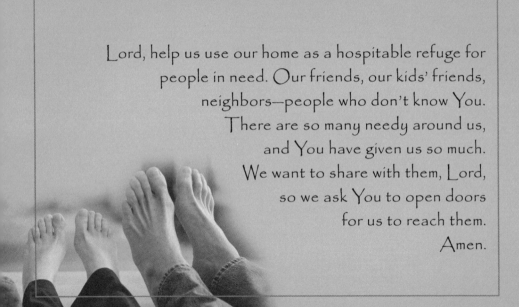

Lord, help us use our home as a hospitable refuge for people in need. Our friends, our kids' friends, neighbors—people who don't know You. There are so many needy around us, and You have given us so much. We want to share with them, Lord, so we ask You to open doors for us to reach them.

Amen.

Lord, I want to hear from You today in a special way. Open my eyes, my heart. Lead me in Your scripture to words meant just for me. Amen.

I'm glad You already know what's in my heart, so when I say I have a hard time trusting You, You aren't surprised. I don't understand Your ways, God, and my heart doesn't always believe what I know with my head—that You are always doing good. Help me trust You more. Amen.

I worry about many things, Lord. No matter how hard I try to let go of my anxiety, it creeps back in. I trust You to take care of me and my needs, Father. Please help me to live out this trust by getting rid of worry in my life. Amen.

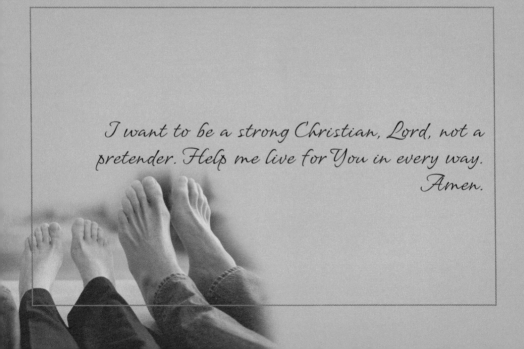

I want to be a strong Christian, Lord, not a pretender. Help me live for You in every way. Amen.

We are, in truth, more than half what we are by imitation. The great point is, to choose good models and to study them with care.

LORD CHESTERFIELD

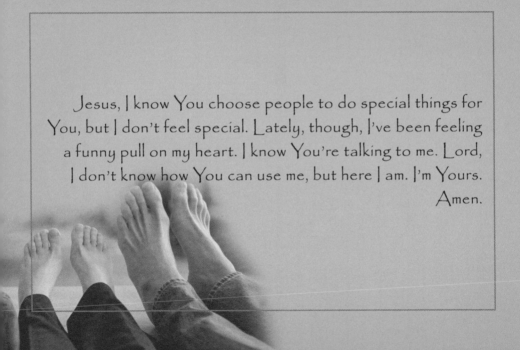

Jesus, I know You choose people to do special things for You, but I don't feel special. Lately, though, I've been feeling a funny pull on my heart. I know You're talking to me. Lord, I don't know how You can use me, but here I am. I'm Yours.

Amen.

The world of entertainment is so enticing, Lord.
Satan knows how to make sin look inviting.
He knows how to trick us into thinking a little won't hurt.
Father God, help us stay strong in our convictions.
Help us make good entertainment choices and teach
our kids to do the same. We need Your help, Lord.
We cannot do this alone.
Amen.

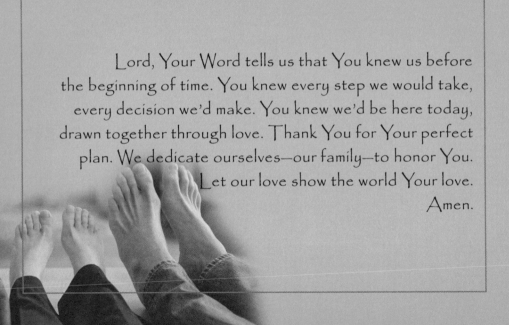

Lord, Your Word tells us that You knew us before the beginning of time. You knew every step we would take, every decision we'd make. You knew we'd be here today, drawn together through love. Thank You for Your perfect plan. We dedicate ourselves—our family—to honor You. Let our love show the world Your love.

Amen.

God, help me honor my parents.
Amen.

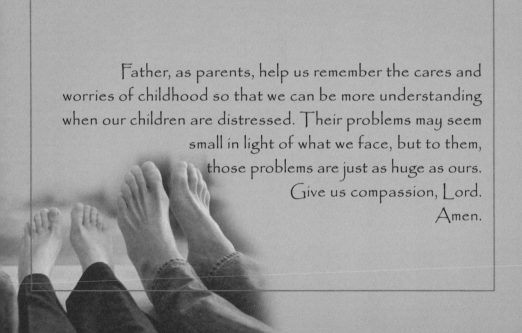

Father, as parents, help us remember the cares and worries of childhood so that we can be more understanding when our children are distressed. Their problems may seem small in light of what we face, but to them, those problems are just as huge as ours. Give us compassion, Lord. Amen.

Every day is a new opportunity to learn more about You, God! Please show us new ways to understand Your love and Your will for our family in our interactions and daily tasks. Amen.

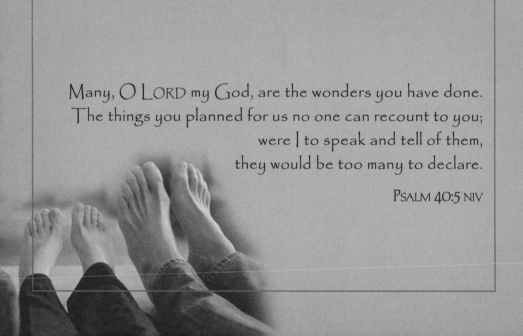

Many, O LORD my God, are the wonders you have done.
The things you planned for us no one can recount to you;
were I to speak and tell of them,
they would be too many to declare.

PSALM 40:5 NIV

Thank You for loving us, Lord, even when we mess up.
We do not deserve Your mercy, yet You give it freely.
We love You, Lord.
Amen.

Jesus, I'm so glad You showed us
Your love for children.
Help me to love my kids the way
You do, unconditionally,
no matter what they do.
Amen.

God, sometimes it's hard to let go of past hurts.
But I know that You don't want me to hold a grudge.
Help me to forgive the people who have hurt me,
and please forgive me for harboring this hurt in my heart.
Amen.

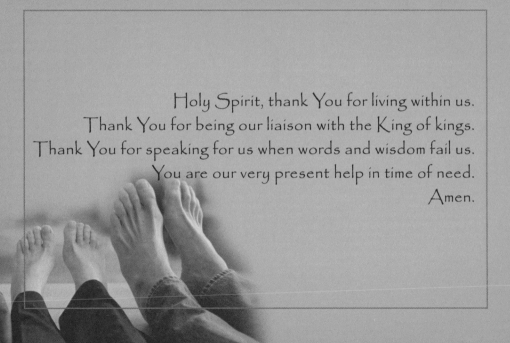

Holy Spirit, thank You for living within us.
Thank You for being our liaison with the King of kings.
Thank You for speaking for us when words and wisdom fail us.
You are our very present help in time of need.

Amen.

Jesus, sometimes it seems like it's easier to hurt other people instead of being nice. Help me to remember that my example is important. When others look at me, they need to see You. Amen.

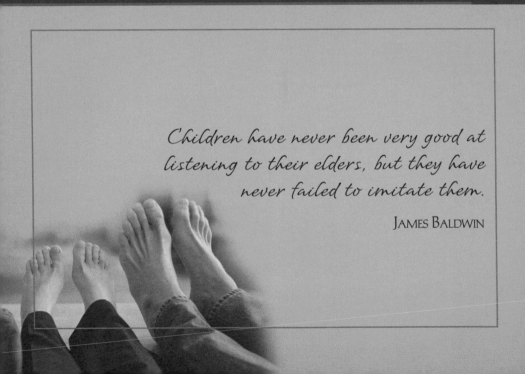

Children have never been very good at listening to their elders, but they have never failed to imitate them.

James Baldwin

Lord, I looked at my almost-grown child today and I was so blessed. I remember those first moments, those first years. Where has the time gone? How did this baby get so grown-up? But I look in his eyes, Lord, and I see You. Thank You for the man my son is becoming. Keep him close to You, even as he begins to move away from us.

Amen.

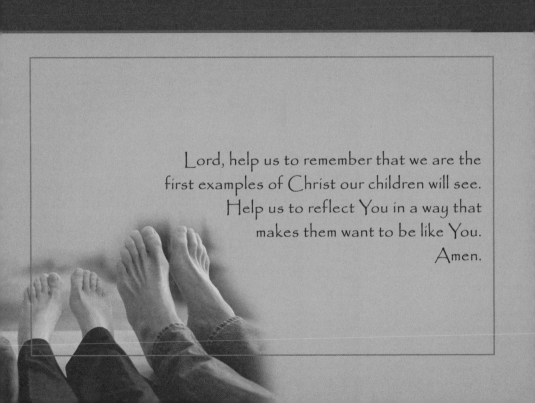

Lord, help us to remember that we are the
first examples of Christ our children will see.
Help us to reflect You in a way that
makes them want to be like You.
Amen.

Lord, help me to be a good friend. Help me treat people fairly and honestly. Help me to show love, even when the other person hurts my feelings. Amen.

Dear God, thank You for helping me be brave when I have to do things that aren't easy. Amen.

Lord, there are tons of books out there telling us how to raise our kids. Father, help us remember to turn to Your Word first. It may not always be politically correct, but it will always be the best advice we can find.
Thank You for providing.
Amen.

Wives, understand and support your husbands in ways that show your support for Christ. The husband provides leadership to his wife the way Christ does to his church, not by domineering but by cherishing. So just as the church submits to Christ as he exercises such leadership, wives should likewise submit to their husbands.

EPHESIANS 5:22-24 MSG

Lord, I know You do not sleep—You are ever watchful over Your children. Thank You for Your vigilance and Your love. We can be strong and confident because of it.

Amen.

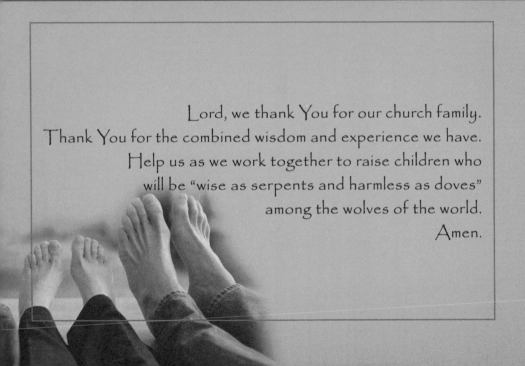

Lord, we thank You for our church family.
Thank You for the combined wisdom and experience we have.
Help us as we work together to raise children who
will be "wise as serpents and harmless as doves"
among the wolves of the world.
Amen.

Father God, we're going through a tough time right now, but we know it's part of Your plan. Try us and purify us, Lord. Like Job, let us come out of this experience as pure gold. Amen.

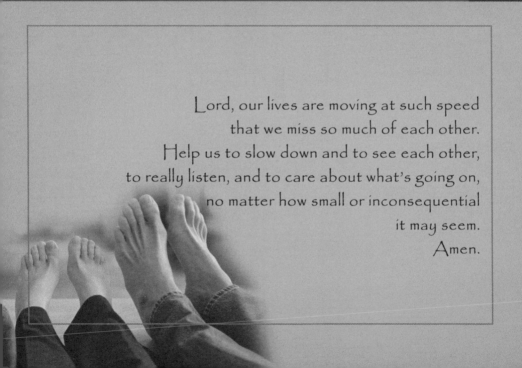

Lord, our lives are moving at such speed
that we miss so much of each other.
Help us to slow down and to see each other,
to really listen, and to care about what's going on,
no matter how small or inconsequential
it may seem.
Amen.

Dear Jesus, thank You for dads.
They're great!
Amen.

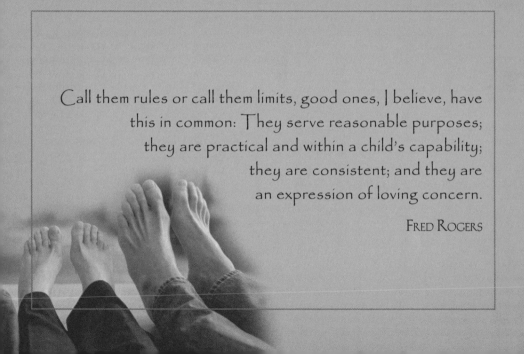

Call them rules or call them limits, good ones, I believe, have this in common: They serve reasonable purposes; they are practical and within a child's capability; they are consistent; and they are an expression of loving concern.

FRED ROGERS

Father, thank You for this beautiful family. As they grow, we pray that each of our children will learn to love and trust You and will accept You as his or her personal Savior. We thank You for the things You will do with and for each of us, Lord. Amen.

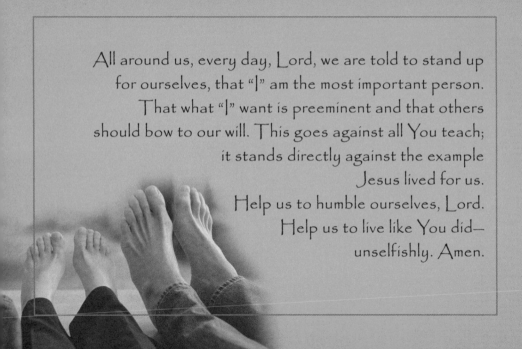

All around us, every day, Lord, we are told to stand up
for ourselves, that "I" am the most important person.
That what "I" want is preeminent and that others
should bow to our will. This goes against all You teach;
it stands directly against the example
Jesus lived for us.
Help us to humble ourselves, Lord.
Help us to live like You did—
unselfishly. Amen.

Father God, thank You for Your provision for our family. You provide everything we need, and we acknowledge Your great goodness. Amen.

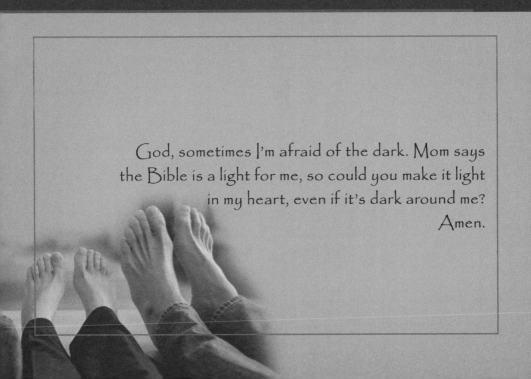

God, sometimes I'm afraid of the dark. Mom says the Bible is a light for me, so could you make it light in my heart, even if it's dark around me?

Amen.

Lord, I don't know how You do it. How do You love us without condition? Sometimes I just don't feel like loving the people You've put in my family. They hurt my feelings, they disrespect me. But I do that to You all the time. O God, I'm sorry! Does the way I act toward You influence their actions toward me?

Lord, help us to practice true love and respect—toward You and each other.

Amen.

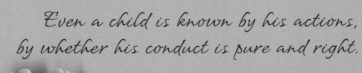

Even a child is known by his actions,
by whether his conduct is pure and right.

PROVERBS 20:11 NIV

Dear God, the chores around the house are never-ending! Please help us to work together as a team to take care of the home You have blessed us with. Amen.

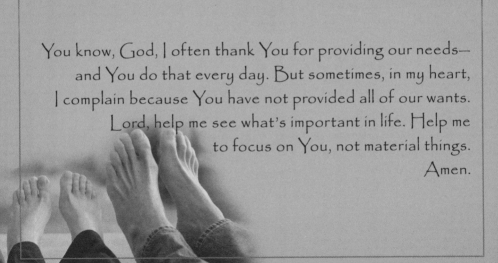

You know, God, I often thank You for providing our needs—
and You do that every day. But sometimes, in my heart,
I complain because You have not provided all of our wants.
Lord, help me see what's important in life. Help me
to focus on You, not material things.
Amen.

God, thank You for giving us the example of fathers that show us a glimpse of the love You offer as our heavenly Father. Please bless the fathers, grandfathers, and male mentors that are in our lives.

Amen.

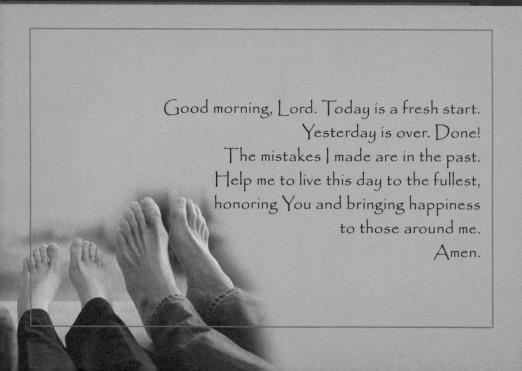

Good morning, Lord. Today is a fresh start.
Yesterday is over. Done!
The mistakes I made are in the past.
Help me to live this day to the fullest,
honoring You and bringing happiness
to those around me.
Amen.

Lord, there are people everywhere that are discouraged. Please bring me an opportunity today to encourage someone else.
Amen.

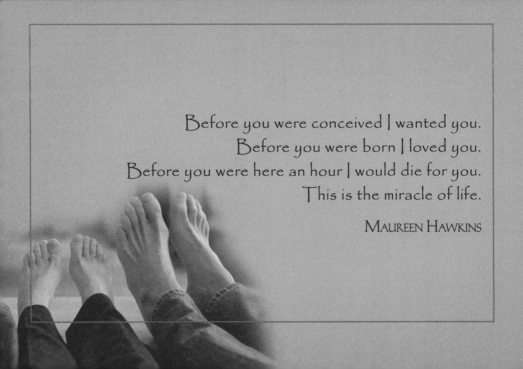

Before you were conceived I wanted you.
Before you were born I loved you.
Before you were here an hour I would die for you.
This is the miracle of life.

MAUREEN HAWKINS

Sometimes, God, we get so busy that we forget to notice the people around us. We take them for granted, especially our family. Help us today to be more aware of each other's feelings and needs. Help us be willing to put our own cares and duties aside to help someone who needs us.
Amen.

Dear God, when someone hurts my feelings,
I need Your help to forgive them.
And when I make a mistake,
thank You for forgiving me!
Amen.

God, it's easy to say I believe in You and that I want to do things Your way, but sometimes, when I'm out with my friends, it's really hard to live what I say. I want to stand up for what I believe, but I'm afraid of what people will think or say about me. Help me to stand, unashamed, for what I know is right. Amen.

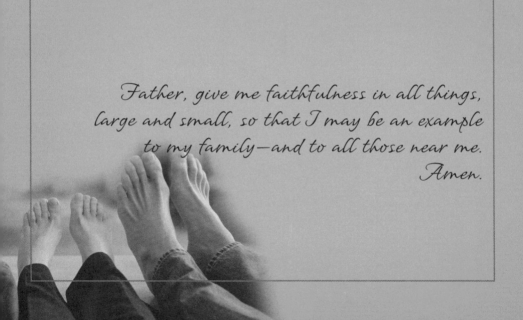

Father, give me faithfulness in all things, large and small, so that I may be an example to my family—and to all those near me.
Amen.

Thank You for granting our request and blessing us with a beautiful family. We give our children back to You, Father. We ask that You would use each one for Your glory. Amen.

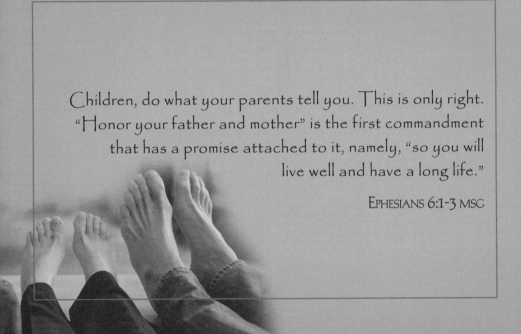

Children, do what your parents tell you. This is only right. "Honor your father and mother" is the first commandment that has a promise attached to it, namely, "so you will live well and have a long life."

EPHESIANS 6:1-3 MSG

Jesus, thank You for the people in our lives that laid the groundwork for the faith our family shares. Grandparents, teachers, ministers, and spiritual mentors offer a rich heritage that we will pass on to future generations—all to Your glory! Amen.

Lord, this parenting thing is hard!
Teach us to be better parents. More loving.
More patient. More understanding.
Help us cuddle when it's needed and discipline
when we should. Help us make good decisions
and smart rules. But most of all, Lord,
help us lead our kids to You, so that
You become their heavenly Father.
Amen.

Heavenly Father, thank You for the ways You show Your love to us. I love seeing Your hand in the tiny details that prove You are completely involved in every moment and every activity in our lives. Thank You for Your constancy. Amen.

God, thank You for Your leading in our lives. Help us to remember to look to You first when making decisions. Amen.

God, You are an amazing God! There is none like You.
Your handiwork surrounds us—in fact, we are Your handiwork,
and we acknowledge Your master craftsmanship.
Amen.

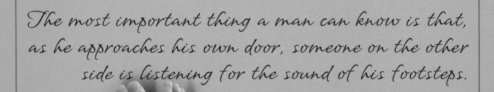

The most important thing a man can know is that, as he approaches his own door, someone on the other side is listening for the sound of his footsteps.

CLARK GABLE

Father, help us to be happy with the way You created us. Each person is different, Lord, but sometimes the urge to conform, to look or act like those around us is so hard to resist. Help our kids realize the value they have in You. Give them confidence in themselves through Your love for them. Amen.

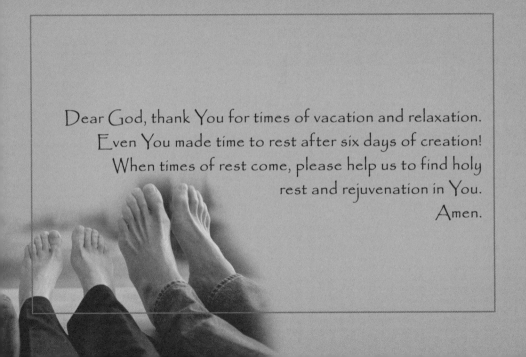

Dear God, thank You for times of vacation and relaxation.
Even You made time to rest after six days of creation!
When times of rest come, please help us to find holy
rest and rejuvenation in You.
Amen.

Father, we have tremendous needs today.
But You, You own the cattle on a thousand hills.
We will trust You to provide our needs.
Thank You, Lord.
Amen.

Dear God, I'm glad You gave me patient parents. They must be a lot like You. Amen.

Lord, I need an attitude adjustment. I've been walking around in a funk for weeks, and I know it's because I haven't spent time in Your Word. Please bless the time I spend today with You in prayer—help me to adopt Your attitude. Amen.

Only be careful, and watch yourselves closely so that you do not forget the things your eyes have seen or let them slip from your heart as long as you live. Teach them to your children and to their children after them.

DEUTERONOMY 4:9 NIV

Lord, our talents are not for our benefit alone.
Help us to consider our abilities as gifts we can give to You.
Thank You for providing us with the perfect way to honor
You—by giving back to You what You provide.
Amen.

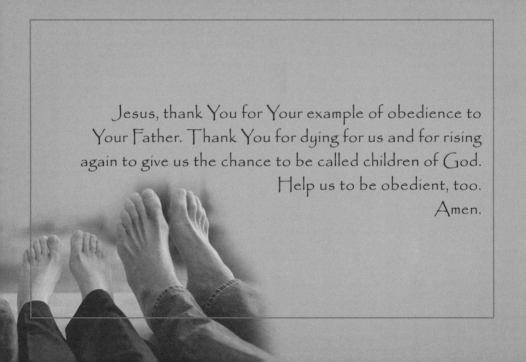

Jesus, thank You for Your example of obedience to Your Father. Thank You for dying for us and for rising again to give us the chance to be called children of God. Help us to be obedient, too.

Amen.

Father God, thank You for answered prayer.
You come through for us every day, and we acknowledge that it is through Your mercy and love that we exist and prosper and, yes, survive.
Amen.

Dear Jesus, thank You for pets.
They're great!
Amen.

Thank You, Father, for this family You have created.
Keep the cords of love here strong and tight.
Help us to love each other like You love us.
Amen.

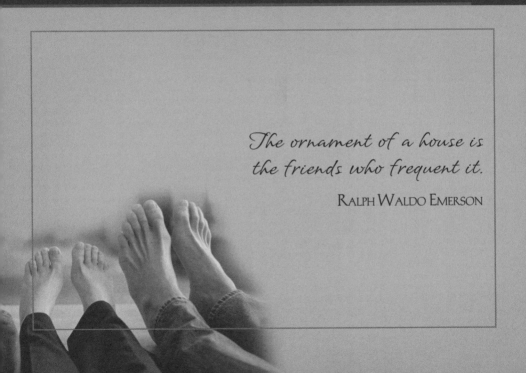

The ornament of a house is
the friends who frequent it.

RALPH WALDO EMERSON

Lord, Your Word says You have set a hedge around us;
You have set Your angels to guard us. We know we are
safe in You and nothing can happen that You do not allow.
Thank You for Your protection.
Amen.

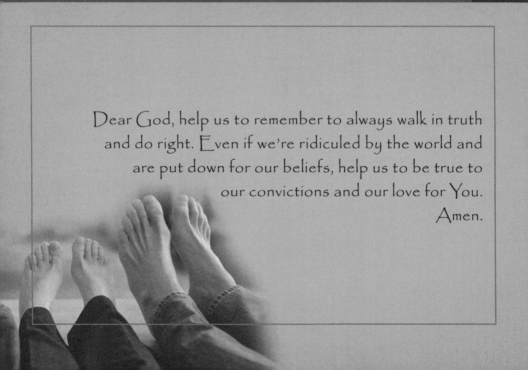

Dear God, help us to remember to always walk in truth and do right. Even if we're ridiculed by the world and are put down for our beliefs, help us to be true to our convictions and our love for You.

Amen.

Jesus, I belong to You. I want to do what You want me to do. Show me Your will. Amen.

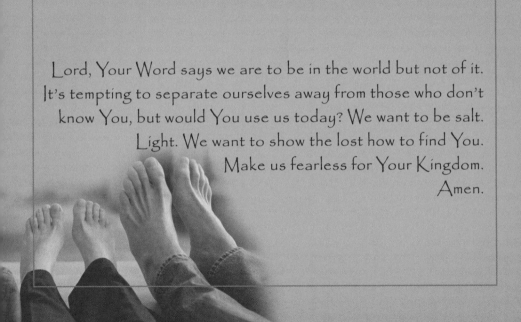

Lord, Your Word says we are to be in the world but not of it. It's tempting to separate ourselves away from those who don't know You, but would You use us today? We want to be salt. Light. We want to show the lost how to find You. Make us fearless for Your Kingdom. Amen.

Lord, You can do the impossible, right?
Would You, please?
Amen.

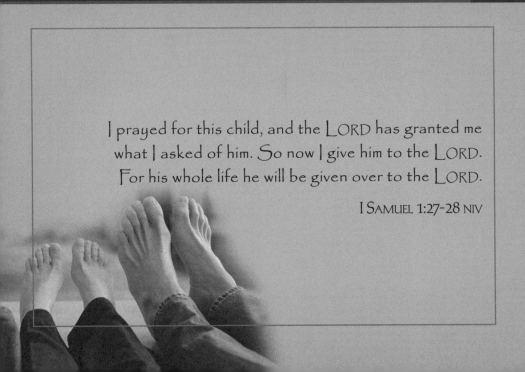

I prayed for this child, and the LORD has granted me
what I asked of him. So now I give him to the LORD.
For his whole life he will be given over to the LORD.

I SAMUEL 1:27-28 NIV

Lord, the material possessions we have are too important to us. The truth is that everything we call ours is really Yours—You just let us use it. Please help us to be good stewards with all our blessings. Help us to see the opportunities to use our money and possessions to help others and glorify You. Amen.

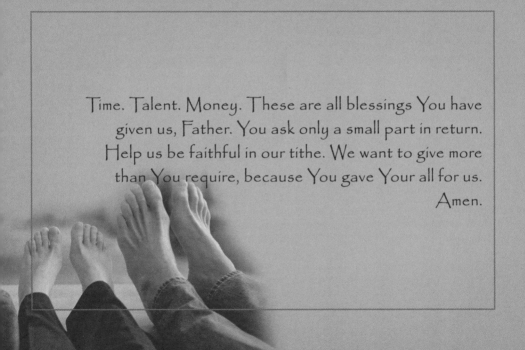

Time. Talent. Money. These are all blessings You have given us, Father. You ask only a small part in return. Help us be faithful in our tithe. We want to give more than You require, because You gave Your all for us.

Amen.

Jesus, thank You that You understand our weaknesses. You have felt fear and temptation and anger. You know the wonder of human joys and the pain of our agonies. Thank You for Your example of faith, even in darkness. Amen.

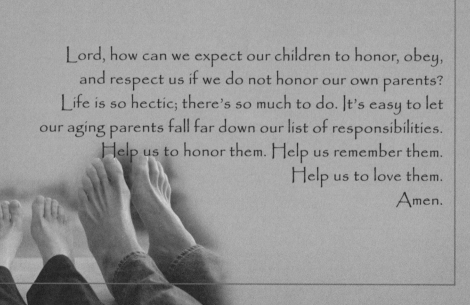

Lord, how can we expect our children to honor, obey, and respect us if we do not honor our own parents? Life is so hectic; there's so much to do. It's easy to let our aging parents fall far down our list of responsibilities. Help us to honor them. Help us remember them. Help us to love them.

Amen.

Dear Jesus, feelings are fragile things.
Help me to remember to be sensitive to others
when they are going through a difficult time.
Amen.

It takes a family to raise a child.

BOB DOLE

God, there are many big decisions in life. When those decisions come, help us to consider everyone involved, but more important, help us to seek Your will. We know You want us to live in Your will, and we want that, too. Amen.

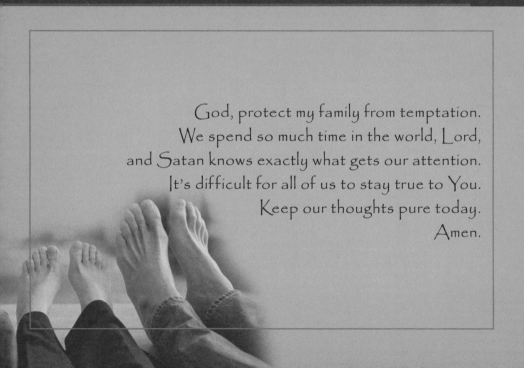

God, protect my family from temptation.
We spend so much time in the world, Lord,
and Satan knows exactly what gets our attention.
It's difficult for all of us to stay true to You.
Keep our thoughts pure today.
Amen.

God, thank You for Your Word. It's amazing to me how a Book written so long ago can be so alive today. How it can speak a word to me, and I know it is from You, for me alone. Thank You!

Amen.

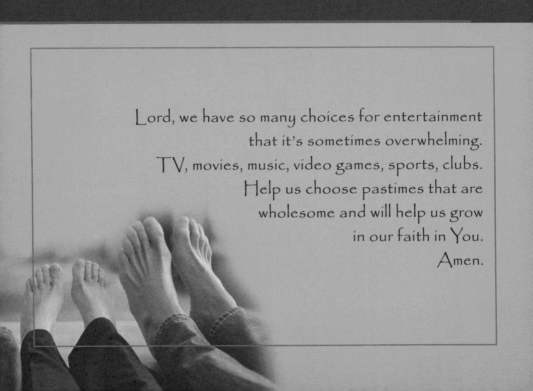

Lord, we have so many choices for entertainment
that it's sometimes overwhelming.
TV, movies, music, video games, sports, clubs.
Help us choose pastimes that are
wholesome and will help us grow
in our faith in You.
Amen.

Father, teach my family to work as a team every day, sharing the good times and the bad, so that none of us should be overburdened. Amen.

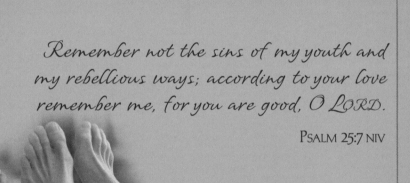

Remember not the sins of my youth and my rebellious ways; according to your love remember me, for you are good, O LORD.

PSALM 25:7 NIV

Father God, how ready You are to help us when we call. Remind us to look to You first when trouble is near.
Amen.

God, why do You allow illness? This is so hard, Lord. We hate to see the pain, the fear, the helplessness on the face of our loved one. Ah! But there is the answer! We are helpless. You are not. Provide healing, Lord. Help us to trust You through this trial.

Amen.

Lord, I did it again. I try so hard to do things right, but then I don't. Help me remember that my strength comes from You, not me. Thank You for forgiving me every time I mess up, even when I do the same things over and over. Amen.

Dear Jesus, sometimes family members don't get along. Sometimes we fight. Please help us communicate in a way that is helpful for the situation and can resolve the conflict quickly.
Amen.

Dear Jesus, thank You for coming into my heart.
I love You!
Amen.

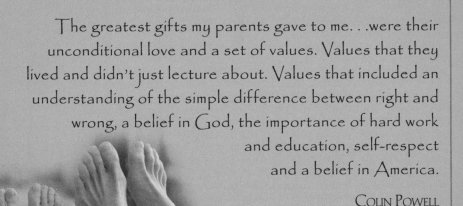

The greatest gifts my parents gave to me. . .were their
unconditional love and a set of values. Values that they
lived and didn't just lecture about. Values that included an
understanding of the simple difference between right and
wrong, a belief in God, the importance of hard work
and education, self-respect
and a belief in America.

COLIN POWELL

Father, I don't see the end of this path we're on. It's dark. It's lonely. It's sad. Please, Abba Father, wrap Your arms around us and show us Your light. Lord, bring good from our situation and use this family to astound the world around us with proof of Your power and glory.

Amen.

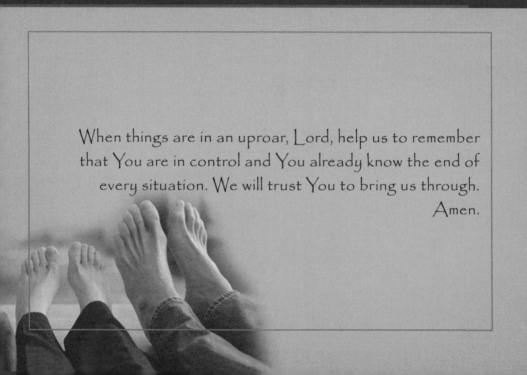

When things are in an uproar, Lord, help us to remember that You are in control and You already know the end of every situation. We will trust You to bring us through. Amen.

Praise loudly; blame softly.

RUSSIAN SAYING

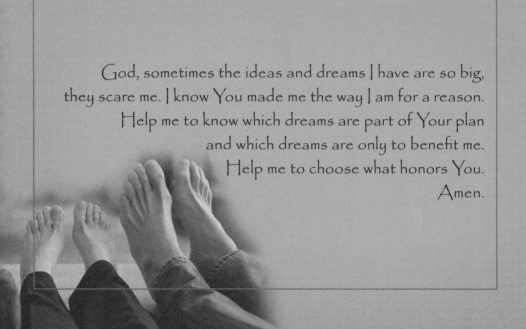

God, sometimes the ideas and dreams I have are so big,
they scare me. I know You made me the way I am for a reason.
Help me to know which dreams are part of Your plan
and which dreams are only to benefit me.
Help me to choose what honors You.
Amen.

Lord, help me to put aside my needs, to draw my child close, and to assure him of my love and, more importantly, of Your love.
Amen.

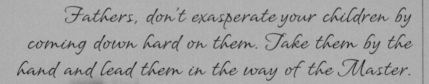

Fathers, don't exasperate your children by coming down hard on them. Take them by the hand and lead them in the way of the Master.

EPHESIANS 6:4 MSG

Lord, remind me to look for You in the everyday.
To see Your beauty in a butterfly, Your majesty
in a snowflake. To recognize Your glory in a song.
Then help me express Your presence to my children,
so they learn to seek You, too.
Amen.

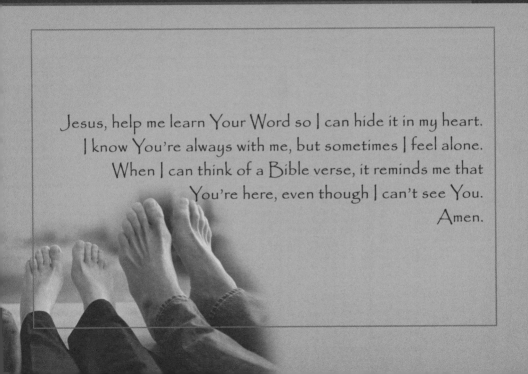

Jesus, help me learn Your Word so I can hide it in my heart. I know You're always with me, but sometimes I feel alone. When I can think of a Bible verse, it reminds me that You're here, even though I can't see You.

Amen.

God, my family cannot come to You through me—the only door is Jesus. I may lead them to the door, but they must choose to enter. Father, give me wisdom, keep me pure so that they want to run to You and not the other way. Amen.

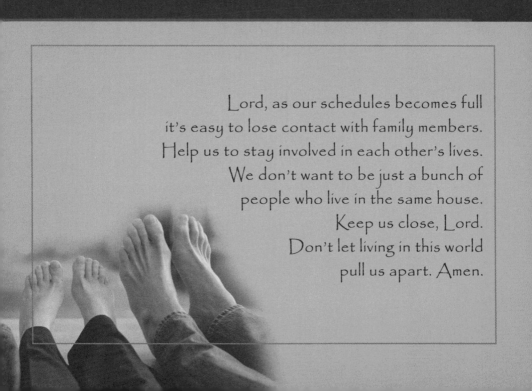

Lord, as our schedules becomes full
it's easy to lose contact with family members.
Help us to stay involved in each other's lives.
We don't want to be just a bunch of
people who live in the same house.
Keep us close, Lord.
Don't let living in this world
pull us apart. Amen.

It is so pretty outside today, God. Thanks for sunshine and nice weather so we can play together! Amen.

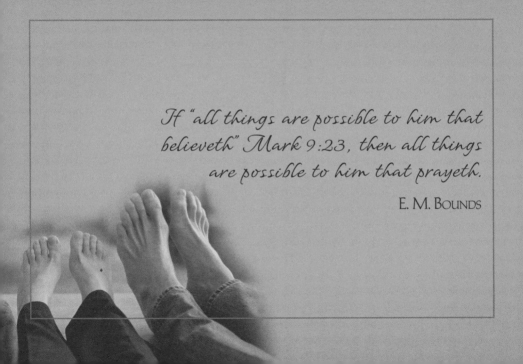

If "all things are possible to him that believeth" Mark 9:23, then all things are possible to him that prayeth.

E. M. BOUNDS

God, You say we should be angry but not sin.
I'm pretty sure I failed on that.
Lord, forgive me for being impatient and selfish.
Forgive me for the way I treated my family members today.
Help me to be more loving and more understanding.
Help me be like You!
Amen.

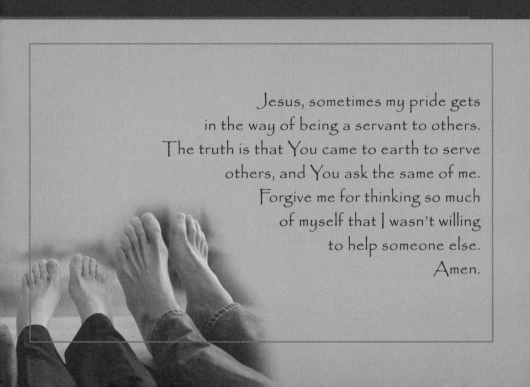

Jesus, sometimes my pride gets
in the way of being a servant to others.
The truth is that You came to earth to serve
others, and You ask the same of me.
Forgive me for thinking so much
of myself that I wasn't willing
to help someone else.
Amen.

Lord, the world today offers so many guilty pleasures. Help us avoid dangerous situations, Lord. Keep our thoughts pure, and when something slips past our defenses, remove it from our minds.

Amen.

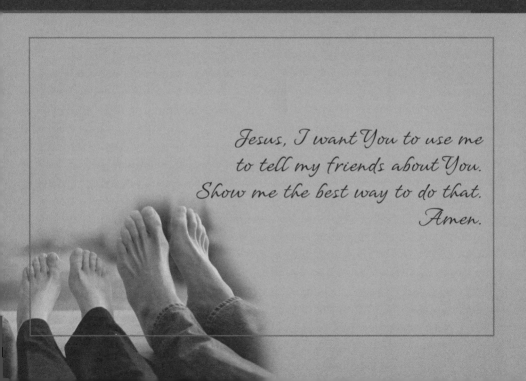

Jesus, I want You to use me
to tell my friends about You.
Show me the best way to do that.
Amen.

Lord, thank You for the door of escape You provided for me today. I was so tempted to do what I knew I shouldn't. But at that last moment, just before I chose to sin, You so obviously opened that door. Thank You for rescuing me from myself! Amen.

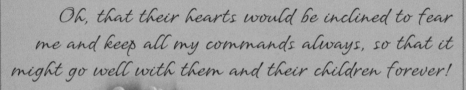

Oh, that their hearts would be inclined to fear me and keep all my commands always, so that it might go well with them and their children forever!

DEUTERONOMY 5:29 NIV

Lord, when we are old, we want our children to respect and love us. By our actions toward others, we are always teaching—either respect or disrespect. We want to set the right example for our children as we honor older people. Amen.

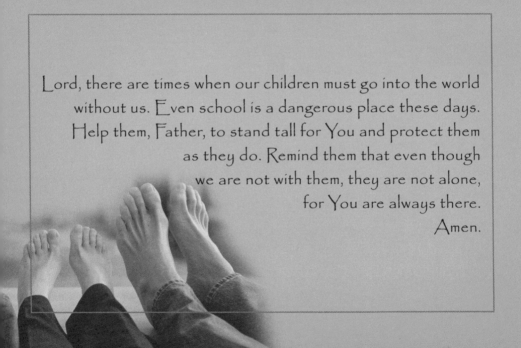

Lord, there are times when our children must go into the world without us. Even school is a dangerous place these days. Help them, Father, to stand tall for You and protect them as they do. Remind them that even though we are not with them, they are not alone, for You are always there.

Amen.

Thank You, Lord, for saving me from myself!
Amen.

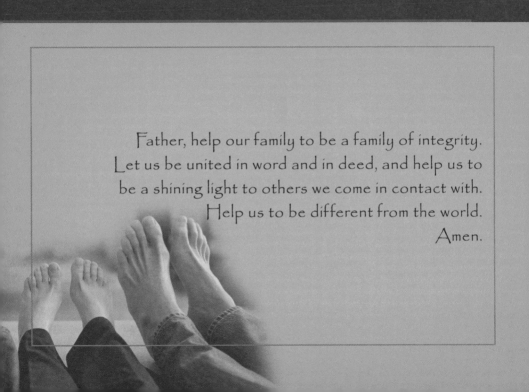

Father, help our family to be a family of integrity. Let us be united in word and in deed, and help us to be a shining light to others we come in contact with. Help us to be different from the world.

Amen.

Jesus, when one of us comes home with a sickness, odds are the whole house will end up with the bug. Please help us to remain healthy, or if we do get sick, help us to serve each other the way You want us to—with patience and understanding. Amen.

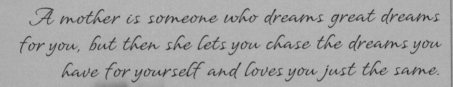

A mother is someone who dreams great dreams for you, but then she lets you chase the dreams you have for yourself and loves you just the same.

UNKNOWN

Lord, thank You for the special friends You have blessed me with. Please help me to strike a good balance between my friend relationships and my family relationships, neglecting neither but nurturing both.
Amen.

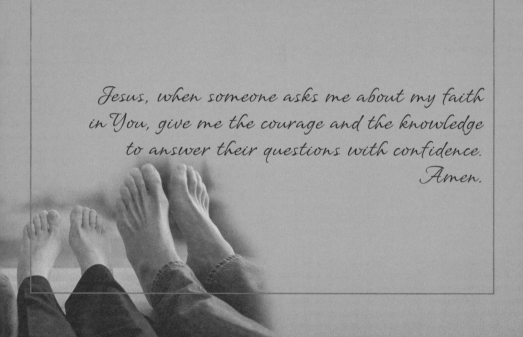

Jesus, when someone asks me about my faith in You, give me the courage and the knowledge to answer their questions with confidence. Amen.

Oh, Father, sometimes it seems easier to be nice to strangers than to the people we love. Help us to appreciate each other. Let familiarity breed respect and understanding, not contempt. Remind us that home should be a place of refuge, not a battlefield. Amen.

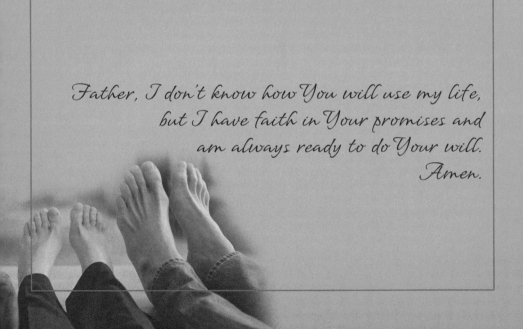

Father, I don't know how You will use my life,
but I have faith in Your promises and
am always ready to do Your will.
Amen.

Lord, help us to teach our children to look through the outward appearance when they choose their friends. Help them see what lies within so they choose wisely. Remind them that they, too, have inward appearances, and help them keep them clean. Amen.

Listen to my prayer, O God,
do not ignore my plea.

PSALM 55:1 NIV

Lord, we all face consequences when we make bad decisions. Help our family to teach lovingly, correct when appropriate and helpful, and extend grace when it is good to do so. Amen.

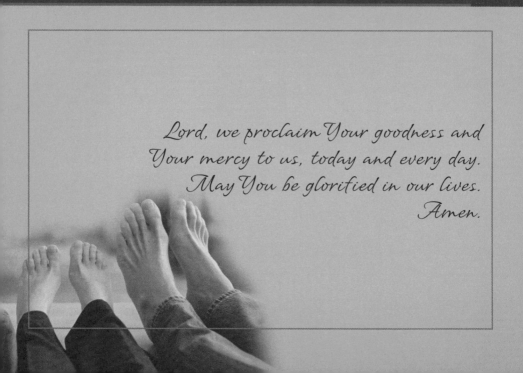

Lord, we proclaim Your goodness and Your mercy to us, today and every day. May You be glorified in our lives. Amen.

Lord, help us to handle money and assets wisely.
We don't always make the best decisions.
You give clear direction—help us choose to follow.
Amen.

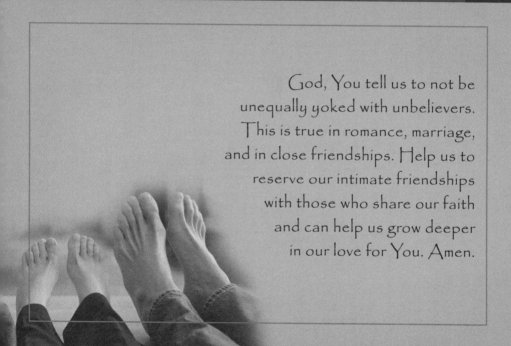

God, You tell us to not be unequally yoked with unbelievers. This is true in romance, marriage, and in close friendships. Help us to reserve our intimate friendships with those who share our faith and can help us grow deeper in our love for You. Amen.

Father, remind us often that all good comes from You.
Don't let us get so caught up in the abilities You have
given us that we forget that without You, we are nothing.
We return to You the gifts You have given us.
Use them for Your glory, Lord.
Amen.

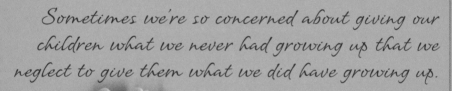

Sometimes we're so concerned about giving our children what we never had growing up that we neglect to give them what we did have growing up.

JAMES DOBSON

Father, I want to make You exciting to my family.

Give me creative ideas as we take walks, clean the house,

do schoolwork, or engage in other routine activities.

I pray it will be a delight for all of us.

Amen.

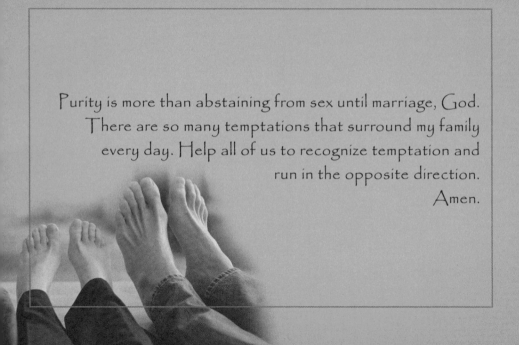

Purity is more than abstaining from sex until marriage, God. There are so many temptations that surround my family every day. Help all of us to recognize temptation and run in the opposite direction.

Amen.

You bless our lives in so many ways every day, Father. May we receive Your blessings with songs of thanksgiving on our lips. Amen.

Dear Jesus, give our family courage to stand for what is good. You are faithful, Lord. We will stand on Your promises. They are Yours. Amen.

Heavenly Father, we want to serve You, but we know we can only do that if we have true faith in You. Help us to live with this kind of faith.

Amen.

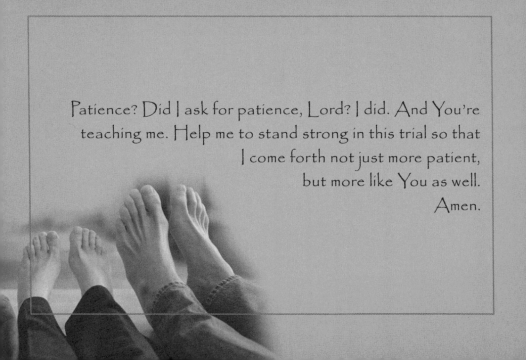

Patience? Did I ask for patience, Lord? I did. And You're teaching me. Help me to stand strong in this trial so that I come forth not just more patient, but more like You as well.

Amen.

"The LORD bless you and keep you; the LORD make his face shine upon you and be gracious to you; the LORD turn his face toward you and give you peace."

NUMBERS 6:24-26 NIV

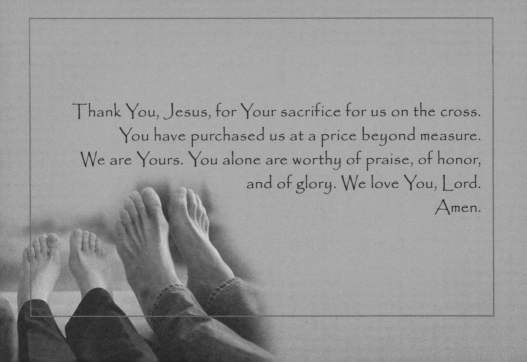

Thank You, Jesus, for Your sacrifice for us on the cross.
You have purchased us at a price beyond measure.
We are Yours. You alone are worthy of praise, of honor,
and of glory. We love You, Lord.
Amen.

Eight days a week I love you.

JOHN LENNON AND PAUL McCARTNEY

Father God, our children are growing up so fast!
Help us to teach them to be independent,
wise in the world, and close to You.
Help us let them go when it's time.
Amen.

Lord, thank You for the beauty of the earth.
Not only did You create us and our present home,
but You made it a nice place to live! I can't wait to
see the beauty of heaven You're preparing!
Amen.

There are wonders in prayer because there are wonders in God.

E. M. BOUNDS